The Bright Side of the Coin

Poetry to make you smile?

Written and illustrated by
Philip L. Ward

To Alicia
I hope it makes you smile.
Thomas xx

Classification: Humorous Poetry

First published 2012
Published in the UK by Inglenook Books
First Edition
Poems and illustrations by © Philip L. Ward
Wilford, Nottingham, UK

ISBN: 978-0-9575136-0-0

All rights reserved. The contents of this book shall not be copied, reproduced, stored on any retrieval system or transmitted in any form without the author's permission.

Printed by Adlard Print and Reprographics,
Ruddington, Nottingham, UK
calvin@adlardprint.com
0044 (0)115 921 4863

Credits

To all my friends and family who gave me the inspiration and encouragement to write this book.

A few of these poems are modelled on some
very special people.
You know who you are or can hazard a good guess.

Sue for my proofreading.

Alex for the cover picture.

Brittney Murphy for the use of the Writing Stuff font.

CONTENTS

Chocolate Vampire	1
Seagulls	2
Daddy's Boy Andrew	4
An Enjoyable Smoke	6
Bed and Breakfast	7
Calibre Girls	8
Sod the Chancellor	9
Chain Smoking Slob	10
The Worries of Folk	11
Feeling Great	12
To be an Ant	13
My Comfort Blanket	14
Mona Long's Lots	15
Can You Lend Me?	16
Stoking for a Date	18
We are not Amused	20
You Can't Win	21
Back in the Black	22
Life of a Dung Beetle	25
The UHU Curse	26
Ode to Idleness	28
Shocking	29
Harry the Fish	30
Blowing my Mind	31
A "Dicky" Seaman	32
Pushing the Boundaries	34
Unwanted Tenant	37
The Accident	38
St. Michael	39
Consequences	40
Tanning	41
Sunday Morning	42
A Judge's Lament	43
Ecstasy	44

Madam Zarla	45
The Misunderstanding	46
Midnight Raid	47
Getting My Own Back	48
Life's Twists and Turns	49
Taking Care of my Hair	52
Devotion	53
Gasping	54
Our Pet's Pets	55
Inconsideration	56
An Armchair Conversation	57
Jim	59
Taking the Hiss	60
A Church Farce Saga	61
Your Last Flame	66
The Single Handed Sailor	67
Dining in	68
Oh I've got to get Fit	69
The Misunderstanding of Marjorie Cleese	72
The Village Pub	74
In Hindsight	76
Second Thoughts	78
A Hole in One	79
Bionic Geriatricism	80
Spider	82
Happiness	83
Between the Posts	84
Contentment	86
Caught in the Act	87
Ronald's New Mac	88
The Ageing Process	90
Couple of Show-offs	91
A Blind Date in Eden	92
Raising an Eyebrow	93

Neighbourhood	94
All Because the Lady Loves Chablis	96
Adolescence	97
Newton's Headache	98
I Love You so Much I Can't be Without You	99
Sharing Their Nuts	100
Naive	101
Old Jake	102
Food Power	103
Sweet Treat	104
Jack & Jill	105
Donation	106
A Golden Opportunity	108
Sunshine for Health	109
Going Nowhere	110
Settling Down	111
Fish Wife	112
Holiday of a Lifetime	114
Gran'd Exit	115
Summer Lottery	116
Oh the Wind	118
Bacon	119
Retribution	120
Geri's Outing to Blackpool	122
Halloween Madness	124
Justice on the Rebound	126
Table Differences	128
Miss Broken Hart	129
Not the Way	130
Life in School	132
Scrambled Egg on Toast	133
Not All There	134
A Dogs Dream of Winning the Lottery	136
Going Fishing	137

Time for Nothing 138
Endorsed by Larva 139
Divine Light 140
I'm Fired 141
Pushing the Wrong Button 142
Did you Know? 143
Hopping the Boards 144
Sport for All 145
How Much Longer Jim? 146
Inheritance 148
Epilogue 149

FOREWORD

As a boy I remember my mother reading comic verse to me. I think it was an attempt to interest me in reading. I hated reading and thought television and especially cartoons were the soul of life. I used to think that nothing else would ever entertain me so much. How wrong I was, and just as I grew out of thinking that the only food worth eating was baked beans so I grew out of cartoons.

Through life I have been influenced by many things, some of them small and insignificant, but they have had as much effect on me as the milestones. One of them a poem by Hilaire Belloc called Henry King comically describes in verse how a boy dies from eating bits of string. How idiotic, but extremely encapsulating and memorable, much more memorable than quoting Wordsworth and Masefield at school. Don't get me wrong I love Wordsworth and Masefield but I can remember the words of the funny poems much easier than I can the classics. It's a bit like pop groups and classical music. Most people remember the songs groups sang but ask them about the classical composers and what they wrote, and the response will be quite different. What interests the mind sinks in and in my case it was the lighter more humorous events.

Over the years in times of emotion I have put pen to paper and written poetry to distract myself from the upheavals I was experiencing at the time. Then one day as I was clearing out some old papers I came across some of my previous attempts at poetry and I reminiscently spent a while reading them. The feeling to write poetry was back but in a different way. I wanted to make fun of everyday life and objects, to see the amusing side and put it into verse. I am naturally light hearted and often reprimanded for it mainly by members of my family. They tell me to take life more seriously. Why, I ask myself? Let me see the funny side of life. I'll never change.

This collection of poems reflects over thirty years of thoughts and writings. There are many more and I will reserve them for another time.

Please enjoy this read and tell your friends. Even buy another copy and give it to them for a birthday or Christmas present.

Make my day as I make yours.

Chocolate Vampire

The dark and white a lovely sight, a sneaky bite to eat at night,
When I'm at home and on my own I must condone my little groan
of pleasure as the smell of it comes face to face with my lips,
Then disappears without a trace through the hole within my face.
I lay there quite contentedly in my state of ecstasy,
From the pleasure I'd assumed was from the food I'd just consumed,
Or was it my mind's giddiness from my new found happiness,
The lovely feel of naughtiness weakened by my willingness
to self indulge in my desire of what my body does inspire,
Necessity to require.
I'm just a chocolate vampire.

Seagulls

I don't have to tell you what happened next,
I walked into an ambush it wasn't my fault,
Strolling the prom with a big bag of chips,
That's when it happened 'The Seagull Assault'.

If they are prepared to fight for my snack,
They've pecked off more than they can chew,
I'm armed and I'll give them one hell of a whack,
I'll show them what's what with the heel of my shoe.

There's more of them now the word has got round,
I'm out in the open and feeling quite stuck,
It's one against fifty I'm standing my ground,
Sure that I'm anxious I'm their sitting duck.

Thoughts of the Light Brigade come to my mind,
With a change to the outcome I'm making my stand,
Preparing for battle for the sake of mankind,
The gulls and me I wait the command.

Off comes my shoe and I'm ready for action,
What happens next I observe with dismay,
The smell of my feet was the cause of distraction,
The pong was so bad that they all flew away.

Daddy's Boy Andrew

Andrew was a Brylcreem boy a product of the fifties,
His Dad would slap it on his head to make his son look smart,
Short back and sides was the cut he never knew the difference,
He was his father's pride and joy and had to look the part.

Thirty years and nothing changed his friends they didn't half rib him,
His lack of understanding of how hair styles now had changed,
So they hatched a plot to help him come to terms with modern living,
You never know who he might meet if things were rearranged.

They'd ask him how he was each day and hide a little snigger,
The plan in place they couldn't wait to know what's going on,
Then one day when he met them he wore a brand new beret,
Things had changed they knew it from what obviously had gone.

My hair's dropped out he told them quite discreetly in a panic,
I went to comb it, off it came as if I'd worn a rug,
There it was all in my hand I stared and couldn't believe it,
I wasn't heavy handed, only gave a little tug.

Weeks went by and shoots appeared it was a lighter colour,
He combed it back the modern way he was a top film star,
Now confident and popular he was the ladies favourite,
We never told him that we'd put remover in his jar.

An Enjoyable Smoke

A good shag in the morning,
Three nuns I love at night,
There's nothing like a nice cool pipe
to round the day off right.
I love the smell of backy,
I use it every day,
Smoking helps relax me
and it takes my cares away.

Bed and Breakfast

Can I take your order sir?
Standing there with a notepad her
apron ready for the task
of getting me some breakfast.

Continental or a fry
or something else you'd rather try,
Tea or coffee, toast brown or white
conjures up a welcome sight.

M'mm the bacon and the toast,
Equivalent to the Sunday roast,
What a way to start the day,
Shame it's not a holiday.

Calibre Girls

*Written for the girls of Calibre talking books on
arriving just on time for an exhibition one day.*

Wow just made it, come on Nic that's our table over there,
Get the stuff out make it quick I've just got time to brush my hair,
I am Nic and this is Lily we're the girls to help you out,
With a service really friendly that's what our jobs all about,
Talking books is our business, read by famous people we
lend them out to all our members who find it really hard to see,
Novels, poetry, plays and humour anything you want or need,
Many titles, many authors it just depends on what you read.

Sod the Chancellor

From 16 to 60 I paid my tax,
From 60 onwards I'm clawing it back,
I'm opting out of your rat race,
To disappear without a trace.

So I'm saying up yours and I don't give a damn,
The feeling I have is that life is a sham,
You line all your pockets with my hard earned loot,
So I'm doing a bunk and I don't give a hoot.

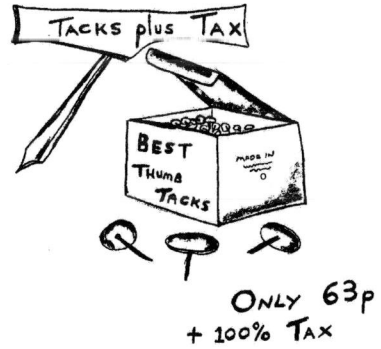

Chain Smoking Slob

Giz a fag I'm gasping an I really an't a clue,
Why ya dint offer, well I spose that's just loik you,
Kunt you see I need one look me face its turnin red,
There's y'r packet on the teble, go git on out of bed.
Ow cum you've always got some where'd ya git the dosh?
I think ya ought to giv em up 'n giv mi better nosh,
I swere these fags are smaller they've cut down on the length,
Not like the ones me faver smoked, no filters and full strength.

Ahhh,

Now that's much better me first drags always best,
Don't bover with the ash tray I'll catch it in me vest,
So what, its aff past midnight I couldn't git to sleep,
You're ok I know you are I erd ya counting sheep.

Naa,

I'm not addicted Ik'n giv up any time,
Mebe I'll try lighter brands and ditch the old Woodbine.

Cough?

Naa,

Its nuffin special I've ad it ages now,
'n I'm fit as a fiddle and still wokking not like yow,
So pack in avin a go at mi an let me av me kip,
Just butt'n it and lev it out, 'n no more of ya lip.

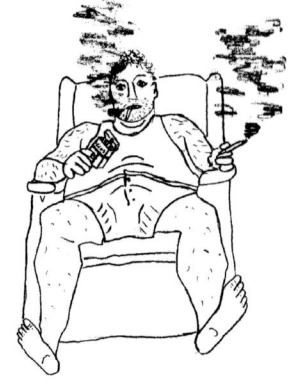

The Worries of Folk

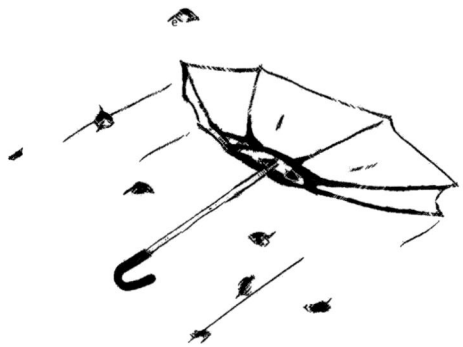

Where's me umbrella I had it in me hand,
I can't lose that, I borrowed it she'll throw a dicky and
if I don't return it in the state she gev it me,
I'll git no snap for me lunch and nuffing for me tea.

Feeling Great

Reach high, touch the sky,
Punch the air like you don't care,
Ask me why I feel so good,
And I'd tell you if I could,
Life is great and it won't wait,
So come with me and celebrate.

To be an Ant

If I were an ant
I'd be elegant
and mix with royalty,
I'd dress real fine
and outrageously dine
on caviar and brie.
I'd be a gentleman worker
and pander to the queen,
I'm just a throw back from my past
a hope that might have been.
I watch the ants with wonder
and wish that it was me,
With delusions of great grandeur,
Aspirations of a flea.

My Comfort Blanket

On a cold and frosty winters night,
There's nothing more than I desire,
To wrap a blanket good and tight,
Around me sat before the fire
and stare upon the amber glow
in wonder as the dancers weave,
A merry reel of make believe.

Mona Long's Lots

Mona had a good voice she was an auctioneer,
She'd sing the bids out for the lots,
This made the punters cheer.

At weekends she was busy she'd joined the local choir,
She sang with the sopranos and could sing an octave higher.

They chose her for the talent show to represent the town,
She didn't win, a violin, walked off with the crown,

So she got herself an agent and hoping for that break,
Invited scouts from Music Mag that was her big mistake.

She wanted to be famous and thought that she could sing,
It didn't help, the critics wrote: "She made our ears ring".

A lighthouse asked her for some help, a job, what did she think.
Their foghorn unreliable was often on the blink.

Poor Mona Long was shattered, reviews rang out bad news,
She sank into depression a bad case of the blues.

She's now down at her auction house a noted rising star,
Singing bids on all her lots strumming an old guitar.

Can You Lend Me?

Can you lend me a quid Sid?
I'm a bit short of funds at the moment,
It'd make me really happy if you did,
It may not be a lot to you but if you only knew
how much a quid means to me.
Then you'll see that with that nice round pound,
I can get a round of beans on toast with a roast or two for free
and a tea, gee what a quid means to me.

Can you lend me a fiver Luv?
Honest Gov I'm not a skiver and I don't do drugs either,
I need a sub till I can get down to the pub,
Where my mates owe me twenty and that's plenty
to pay you back and have some left over.
It's no bother if you won't
and I'll not pester you if you don't,
But there'll be no food for the kids or their mother.

Can you lend me a ton Hun?
I've had a terrible day where nothings gone my way
and I need some fun,
So I'm off down the casino to have a beano,
With my girl Shirl, she's a real pearl
to hurl some dice and it'd be nice
when all's said and done to have come out and won,
A tidy sum.

Can I tap you for a grand Stan?

I'll pay you back as soon as I can and

you can have my Rolex till Friday,

That's the day I get my pay, what'd say?

I need it now to buy a car,

Lend it to me, be a star,

That's what you are,

Best mate by far.

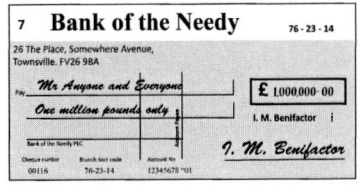

Hi Rich can you lend me a mill,

I promise I will, always fly on your airlines

at the times I need to nip off to the States,

I know that your rates are really great,

So please don't hesitate mate,

You'll get it back with interest,

Honest,

I can't wait.

Stoking for a Date

Max Casson was a stoker
and very good at that,
He'd stoke the barges up the Thames,
Then stoke them coming back.

He had muscles on his muscles,
A truly great physique,
Not only could he shift the coal
he could do it double quick.

The ladies up the mews at home
all hoped their cards were marked,
And thought it was significant
whose house outside he'd parked.

He'd do their little jobs for them,
He really was quite handy,
It got them hot and bothered
not to mention very randy.

A stoker for a partner,
What girl could want for more?
A fit and active husband,
At least to sixty four.

But Max's thoughts were elsewhere,
He had his eye on Cecil,
The one who he's been stoking for,
The captain of the vessel.

We are not Amused

I'm not sure if it's fact or rumour
Queen Victoria lost her humour,
Deciding one day she refused,
All attempts to be amused.

Some say it was indigestion,
Others claim that's speculation,
I believe what's widely known,
That she hurt her funny bone.

You Can't Win

When I was a baby I couldn't talk,
A few months later I managed a squawk,
I learnt the few words you taught me to say,
You encouraged my learning every day,
I was speaking by two you were over the moon,
And soon after that I sang my first tune,
I was up on my feet and walking was fun,
You helped me with that and taught me to run,
I loved all the things you helped me to do,
Playing an instrument, tying my shoe,
Now that I'm older and wanting to play,
Sit down and shut up is all that you say.

Back in the Black

John would look in the mirror and stare
at the thinning of his hair,
Making wishes, needs and wants,
For a thatch upon his bonce.

How can someone as young as he,
Be accepted seriously,
When all the hair above his face,
Retreated at a galloping pace.

Then all at once he had this thought,
If a dark patch could be bought,
In his pocket he'd carry a comb,
If something lived upon his dome.

So off in search of knowledge new,
And seek advice from folk he knew,
Of what they thought that he should do,
He'd get himself his first tattoo.

It would show that he's a man,
And look the part as best he can,
Suave, distinguished head held high,
He wouldn't need to be so shy.

As the work was going on,
An old fedora he did don,
To hide away from prying eyes,
What would be his great surprise.

His head now done it was fantastic,
Hair pulled forward with elastic,
But it wasn't hair anew,
Just a massive black tattoo.

To hide what once was white and pink,
Pretty good what do you think?
Instead of what was smooth and bare,
Was sporting his new barnet fair.

Now he struts around the town,
Showing off what's on his crown,
All he has to now remember,
Is that date in late September.

When his head would show the sign,
Of that funny growing line,
Where the hair just didn't sprout,
And looked as though the tide was out.

That's the time he goes on back,
For a top-up of the black,
And browse the coiffure books a while,
Seeking out the latest style.

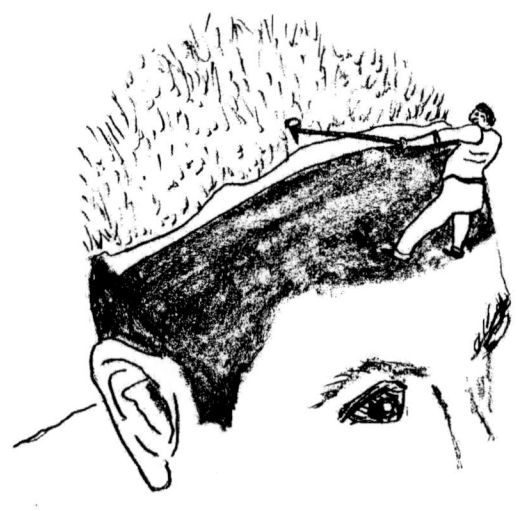

Life of a Dung Beetle

I don't know why I do it?
My job, it don't half stink,
I really have no option,
No matter what you think.
I kick it with my back legs,
You may well ask me why?
To get as far away from it,
'Cos the smell just gets me high.
I roll it for an hour or so,
On the dusty ground,
To knock off all the corners
and to make it nice and round.
This adds an earthy coating,
Like the icing on a cake,
Then I leave it in the sun a while
to leaven and to bake.
You may well ask what happens now,
This ball of dung you see,
Well I bite it into slices
and I have it for my tea.

Later

The UHU Curse

It doesn't matter just how gently
you squeeze a tube of UHU glue,
There always ends up more than plenty,
And it gets all over you.

Besides the table and the chair,
It's on your fingers, in your hair,
It's on your clothes that wretched goo,
It's even worse than doggy poo.

You stuck the thing you bought it for,
You've gone and stuck the kitchen door,
To the packet and the box,
It's even got inside the lock.

There's nowhere now there isn't glue,
You've stuck the carpet to your shoe,
You're firmly fixed and goodness knows,
How it got inside your nose.

Then panic starts to settle in,
It's in your mouth and on your chin,
While summing up the mess construed,
You lose your balance squash the tube.

A jet of nasty sticky stuff,
If all of this was not enough,
Has rained it's droplets through the air,
And scattered almost everywhere.

It's hard to picture at a glance,
If at all there's any chance,
That what has happened here today,
Is down to Karma, me to pay.

For doing something bad before,
To even up and settle a score,
There's nothing I can think that's worse,
Than suffering from the UHU curse.

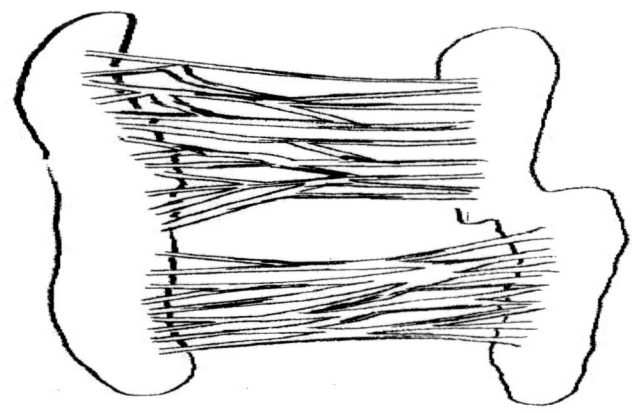

Ode to Idleness

Never let it not be said,
That I like to lie in bed,
Hour on hour I love to laze
and sleep away my working days.

I've heard that it is good for me,
If fit and bright I want to be,
To rest my bones, do what I choose,
That's what I think, it's my excuse.

Now in my easy chair I sit,
Do I regret it? Not a bit?
Old and chilling out for God,
Yes I'm just an idle sod.

Shocking

Funny thing l'ectricity,
You know that it's right there,
But if you try and touch it,
It does strange things to your hair.

Harry the Fish

Harry the fish they called him,
And it was one damp dismal night,
Fit as a fiddle and boy could he swim,
Put up one hell of a fight.

It wasn't me, who caught him,
T'was Johnny from down the MET,
He literally jumped upon him,
Got himself all soaking wet.

You should have seen him wriggle,
An eel he should have been,
We still have a laugh and a giggle,
Remembering the ridiculous scene.

Now down the pub we sometimes meet,
Have a beer with our old skipper,
Telling tales about him on his beat,
And a copper that captured a kipper.

Blowing my Mind

Laying on a red seat,
Sliding off the world,
Flying off to paradise,
Heads all in a whirl.

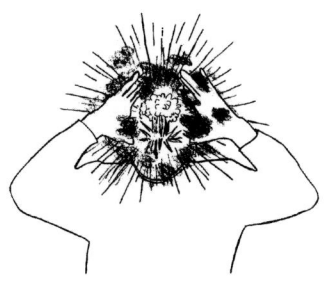

No one's going to know me,
They just don't have a clue,
I'm on another planet,
While I'm inside of you.

What you going to call me,
How you going to know,
Where to post the letter,
Sow, the flowers grow.

Customs men are calling,
They've found me out at last,
Get the cows together,
It'll be a f ****g blast.

I'm going off to somewhere,
For four days five or six,
Don't care about tomorrow,
Now where's my bloody fix?

A "Dicky" Seaman

Going back a year or two,
There was a sailor that I knew,
His name was Tate and what d'you know,
He was a walking picture show.

His name was Tate but not by chance,
And if you stopped to take a glance,
Like many of the people do,
Admire his latest bird tattoo.

Two hundred just upon his arms,
Another twenty on his palms,
They're beak to beak across his chest,
Back and legs you'll find the rest.

They say he's got a goose in flight,
Somewhere hidden out of sight,
An albatross with wings outstretched,
Na, I think that's well far fetched.

When he wears his old string vest,
Aviary! they shout in jest,
In every port he gets one more,
He got a flock in Singapore.

You may think he's raving mad,
And pictured skin is really sad,
But in the end he has this plan,
A very intelligent, astute man.

He'll sell his hide to pay the bill,
Of his impending funeral,
His interest ornithology,
Guaranteed his place in the gallery.

Pushing the Boundaries

T' was Tuesday at the end of May,
With nothing more to do,
While strolling on the beach that day,
That's when the feeling grew.

I'd gone a mile along the sand,
Without a care in mind,
Of all the places in this land,
And not a loo to find.

I tried to just forget it,
And put it out my head,
It didn't help one little bit,
But what was that ahead.

A building in the distance,
It looked a hopeful sight,
Could it be just by chance?
Oh yes, I think it might.

I walked a little faster,
And I whistled as I went,
To take my mind off my state,
And save an accident.

I don't know what is better,
To sprint or take it slow,
At this stage I'll do anything,
To try and stem the flow.

I'm really getting desperate now,
And look around to see,
No shelter, wall or anything,
No bush or even tree.

A couple of minutes longer,
I surely will be there,
A meeting with the porcelain,
Will be a time to share.

A moment of true ecstasy,
Before it is too late,
A feeling I remember,
It won't evaporate.

The place is getting nearer,
It's nothing but a hut,
Exactly what I'm needing now,
Except the sign says shut.

Unwanted Tenant

Before I was evicted
from the place I wasn't wanted,
My landlord wasn't pleased one little bit,
Accused of spying overhead,
At his wife laid out in bed,
She leapt around the room in a screaming fit.

    I know it was predictable,
    Those moments so restrictable,
    A feeling quite collectable,
    In a glass receptacle,

        Lead crystal, how to go in class,
        A perfect piece of fine cut glass,
        Then on the cold wet night time grass.
        He threw me outside on my ass.

The Accident

John never knew what hit him
laying halfway down the street,
He heard a crash and in a flash
he was wiped clean off his feet.
With a funny sense of flying,
Quite a distance from the ground,
And a feeling he was dying,
All was calm, without a sound.
He saw the girl approaching
with a halo round her head,
Then all at once it dawned on him,
He'd expired and he was dead.

St. Michael

St. Michael they all called me,

It wasn't very fair,

Just because my clothes are old and I hadn't combed my hair.

My trousers worn and my shirt is torn,

Vest inside out and back to front,

I must admit I am unkempt,

A proper little runt.

St. Michael they still tease me and I thought it was in jest,

Till I saw it in the mirror,

The label on my vest.

Consequences

The following poem tries to offer a scenario why Quasimodo and Esmeralda never actually got together as a couple.

Quasi met Esmeralda at the annual cathedral fete,
She wasn't wearing any rings so he asked her for a date,
I do like rings she told him I am a girl of taste,
Confused he thought his peal appealed and a smile grew on his face.

Young Quasi was keen to impress her and leapt to the belfry stairs,
So quick was he upon his feet and he took the steps in pairs,
Esi taken back by this asked what was going on?
I've got a small surprise for you, "for me" she said, très bon,

> What happened next was painful,
> That noise was in her head,
> The bells, the bells, oh the bells,
> So she cleared off home instead.

Tanning

When in the mid-day sun,
And you're having lots of fun,
There's one thing that you really ought to learn,
Don't forget those silent beams,
That will penetrate your creams,
And cause your skin to redden and to burn.

Sunday Morning

Laying in bed on a cold Sunday morn,
Open my eyes have a scratch and a yawn,
A packet of biscuits a nice cup of tea,
Then it's off back to bed the cats and me.
Open my book a sip of my tea,
A bite of a Cadbury's chocolate bicky,
Turn a few pages a gulp of tea,
Reaching again for another bicky.
Time drifts by aimlessly,
Involuntary action, another bicky,
Then another bicky and a sip of my tea,
Some pages more the cats and me.
Lying in bed on a Sunday morn,
Stretch out my legs, stifle a yawn,
Biscuits all gone I've finished my tea,
It's time to get up the cats and me.

A Judge's Lament

My body now has had enough,
And working makes me tired,
I've hung my wig upon the peg,
And thoroughly retired.
Not just a case of want to,
Much more than that by far,
The meaning of the words have changed,
Supported by the bar.
Now in my dock I finally lay,
And judgement is upon me,
I've served my sentence, done my time,
Acquitted now quite justly.

Ecstasy

M'mmm the whiff of chips
and associated dips,
Sets your taste buds in spasmodic raptures,
But be careful it's the taste,
That puts weight upon your waist,
So let the smell be all your body captures.

Madam Zarla

Madam Zarla runs the hoopla at the local fair,
And when she's free she's Gypsy Lee with long black raven hair,
She'll tell you what you want to know,
Believe her if you dare,
And if you do well more fool you, you know you should beware,

Cross her palms with silver and she'll claim lucks on its way,
And you'll meet a tall dark stranger;
It's your lucky day.

The Misunderstanding

It was a lovely evening so we chose to have a meal,
At the local eating house they offer a good deal,
My wife had made an effort she wanted to impress,
The waiter even commented on her lovely dress.
The food it looked delicious in fact it smelt divine,
My beef was cooked just perfect and I couldn't wait to dine,
WAITER, pass the mustard please I made it very clear,
I raised my arm and caught his eye I found it hard to hear.
The restaurant was quite crowded so I tweaked my hearing aid,
I'm surprised I could hear anything the noise the people made.
The pot now on the table he asked rhetorically,
Any other condiments sir, ah yes now let me see,
Tell my wife she's beautiful if you'd be so kind,
I know you think that anyway I can almost read your mind.
I beg your pardon sir he said I don't think that is on,
Condiments was what I said, compliments was wrong.

Midnight Raid

The dark of the night and all is still,
I'm wide awake and cannot rest,
Creeping quietly to the kitchen,
Taste buds on their midnight quest,
To satisfy their bid for action,
Through the white door cold and bright,
Heading for the main attraction,
Ice cream for my cellulite.

Getting My Own Back

He opened one hand then the other
and as if by magic it had disappeared,
I hated the tricks performed by my brother,
It's behind my ear again as I feared.

He always likes to do those things to me,
I never seem to live it down,
I'm going to get my own back someday,
Not be treated like some silly clown.

Getting one up on my older brother,
Isn't as easy as I first thought,
Off to the trick shop I went with my mother,
I'll have to hide well the thing that I bought.

Next time he tried it I was ready and waiting,
I could see in his eyes the feeling of pain,
The trick that I bought had snapped on his finger,
He hasn't tried any tricks on me again.

Life's Twists and Turns

Their love could not be stronger,
It stood the test of time,
Happiness reigned longer,
The more their lives entwined.

They even looked alike some said,
From kids when they first met,
And it was no surprise they wed,
A simple life beset.

For thirty years of bliss 'til now,
The children had flown the nest,
Precious extra time'll allow,
The pursuit of other interests.

Inevitability took its course,
And indeed their ways did part,
The lack of understanding forced,
Separation thoughts to start.

Their combined assets weren't enough,
To find another place,
So times in future will be tough,
Austerity to face.

Then thoughts of self preservation,
And what is all involved,
With elaborate plan creation,
To get the whole thing solved.

The neighbours know the problem,
And offer to help out,
With appeals of fairness to them,
And not to scream and shout.

Eventually things turn sour,
She's no longer there,
They're worried by the hour,
The police search everywhere.

He claims she just walked out,
Packed a case and went,
The neighbours seem to doubt,
That it was a non event.

There's now a lot of pressure,
He has to let them know,
Somehow to reassure,
And to make the rumours go.

He's off to go and find her,
And bring her back you see,
To offer a reminder,
Of how things used to be.

To quell the allegation,
Of the people and the press,
And restore his reputation,
Most of all reduce the stress.

She returned alone one day,
He was nowhere to be seen,
It kept the poisoned talk at bay,
From things that might have been.

For many years she lived there,
He never did drop by,
Devoid of friendship and of care,
Maybe he had just died.

She never ever saw him,
The rumours went away,
Life was now worth living,
Parties work and play.

He got just what he wanted,
He was a devious rat,
Thanks to the plastic surgeon,
Who took care of all of that.

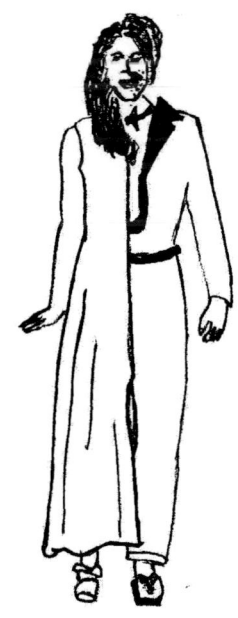

Taking Care of my Hair

I'm off to get my hair cut,
It means a lot to me,
It's the only one that I've got left
so I treat it carefully.
I've had it since my twenties,
It makes me feel a hunk,
I pull the girls with big blonde curls
who like a bit of punk.

Devotion

Outside in the cold, and naked
when I saw you standing there,
Tall and dark and handsome,
With grey in the curls of your hair.

I wanted to stroke and caress you,
Run my fingers through that hair,
Snuggle up close beside you,
We'd make such a lovely pair.

I love the way you tease me,
Leave me gooey and soft inside,
You're always there when I need you,
And I stare at you standing with pride.

I love you loads John Thomas,
You're the only one for me,
I want to wrap myself around you,
And kiss you tenderly.

I'd marry you tomorrow,
If you weren't attached already,
For now it's fine until you're mine,
We'll take it nice and steady.

Gasping

Arid, scorched almost beyond hydration,
A river bed of silt grains and sand,
Waiting for the rains and when it comes,
A long lost friend is greeted.
Embraced with eager arms in haste round and round,
Concerned that they may leave,
Denying refreshment,
Quenching the ribbons carved out
where the last traces of moisture ran,
Drenching that thirst,
At last my throat is alive,
Alive with the first cold beer of the day,
Hooray.

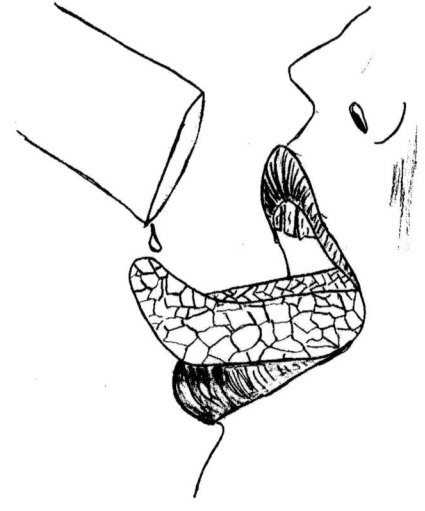

Our Pet's Pets

Suddenly our cat's a spring chicken,
He's leaping about like a kitten,
It seems much more frequent,
The need for some treatment,
The fleas make him jump when he's bitten.

I'm a flea on the back of your cat,
And I'm not very happy with that,
I know I'm not blameless,
But don't make me homeless,
I don't earn enough for a flat.

Well I am the cat in the question,
Trying to make an impression,
There's no bed and breakfast,
For fleas that are downcast,
Regardless that there's a recession.

Inconsideration

The man with the moustache,
He can really make a splash,
When he takes a dive into the deep blue pool,
Other people though,
Try politely not to show,
That his style of entry is certainly not cool.

An Armchair Conversation

Who'll give me 50,
Must be worth 50,
2, 5 and 60,
62,
It's with you,
The lady in blue,
Sold.
Oh, I feel so cheap it makes me weep,
Yes we're old but there's life in us yet,
And don't forget we were the best that you could get,
Mature and tasteful,
A faithful duet.

At least we're together,
We come as a pair,
The finest of leather and softest horse hair,
Upright and straight with a couple of wings,
The things that you get on a very good chair,
Heavy old oak not light as as a feather,
Built for your leisure and ultimate pleasure,
Not MFI
would I lie?
You can always tell our tell-tale smell.

Charles and Henry
they named us when we
were made,
Braid down the side good and wide,
Finished in brass, pure class
and we can tell a tale or two,
If you only knew every ass
that polished our hides,
Gentry to brides,
We've felt them all, the short and the tall.

A chair's an old friend to while away
a lazy day many would say,
So sit for a while and try us out
you'll have no doubt when you're wiped out,
Or take a snooze from too much booze,
Nothing to lose.

We're off to a place to grace the space
in front of an inglenook fireplace.
The best place to be for Henry and me,
Two old boys of antiquity.

Jim

My friend Jim's an alligator,
He's a cartoon animator,
Drawing pictures just for fun,
Sitting outside in the sun,
With his hat on, oh so cool,
Warming gently by the pool,
Another cocktail he would snap,
Certainly is a clever chap.

Taking the Hiss

It's careless really, quite remiss,
For a snake to lose its hiss,
To stick your tongue out with no noise,
Doesn't fit with reptile poise.
On seeing this one might conclude,
That the beast was being rude.

A Church Farce Saga

It happened oh so quickly,
There was no time to run,
The Vicar had never encountered,
A mugger with a gun.

Right outside the church it was,
An hour before the time,
Completely shaken up he was,
But thought that he'd be fine.

Mr Taylor in his Sunday best,
Stood at his pew right proud,
Knowing that others looked up to him,
He stood out in a crowd.

In his jacket and fine white shirt,
Every note he sang in tune,
The model male within his church,
He'd be a saint quite soon.

Not every soul was godly though,
And Billy was one of them,
He'd wipe his nose upon his sleeve,
Then spit out lumps of phlegm.

The Vicar preached a sermon,
On the bad and evil ways,
Of terrorists and madmen,
Heads down, now let us pray.

Today it was a long one,
The Vicar did rant and seethe,
Something had obviously wound him up,
Got the bit between his teeth.

Poor Billy out of boredom,
Started crying and tugging his Mum,
I'm hungry he then said to her,
And proceeded to stick out his tongue.

I've got a homemade sarnie,
She whispered to her son,
Then reached into her handbag,
And handed him the one.

It kept him quiet for quite a while,
The clingfilm was a fight,
He held it in his dirty hands,
And took a massive bite.

Then Billy turned towards his Mum,
And gaped at her mouth wide,
She turned away disgusted,
At what she saw inside?

He didn't like the beetroot,
And turned to tell her clear,
But as he held his head up,
The contents disappeared.

Young Billy coughed and spluttered,
He couldn't catch his breath,
His mother began to panic ,
At Billy's impending death.

A neighbour then reached over,
And grabbed him round his chest,
The Heimlich method I think it was,
Who cares he did his best.

He held him tight and squeezed him,
A pop was all t'was heard,
The contrast with the silence,
Was almost quite absurd.

It worked and Billy was ok,
He sat down quiet instead,
But everyone was still on edge,
From what the Vicar said.

There was an air of tension,
Not relaxed at all,
Though something was going to happen,
And then there was a call.

I'm shot cried Taylor going down,
Blood pouring from his chest,
The organist fell off her stool,
When she saw his reddened vest.

The Vicar was in a frenzy,
Sprinting up the aisle,
Frock all round his ankles,
Completely lacking style.

Get down someone shouted,
We have a madman here,
Better do what he says,
Else he'll kill us all I fear.

Then all at once things settled,
And quiet once more did reign,
The Vicar stopped racing round the church,
And composed himself again.

Young Billy now feeling better,
Not bored at all by this,
Excited by the action,
At what was now amiss.

Old Taylor gasping loudly,
Was prostrate on the floor,
Where was that evil gunman?
Then a noise heard from the door.

Shouted, here! I am a doctor,
I heard a man's been shot,
Now where's the wounded person?
Does it hurt a lot?

I'm dying said old Taylor,
I haven't long to go,
Said with melodramatic conviction,
He was an actor once you know.

Let me see this wound of yours,
Struth everything is red,
I'll have to open up your shirt,
The paramedic said.

An expert in his profession,
Exceptionally astute,
Removed the offending object,
A lump of cooked beetroot.

Your Last Flame

Although my home was no bigger than a box
you always claimed I was your perfect match.
You took me out a few times but nothing came of it,
Then the last time,
You forcibly removed me and struck me on the head.
I was alight with rage,
Why?
Was I just your latest flame?
You used me!
You used me and because of it I burnt myself out.
Now I'm no use to anyone,
Discarded like an old match.

The Single Handed Sailor

I am the intrepid sailor and I cruise the open sea,
I sail the way the wind blows but it's all the same to me,
What people think I do aboard come day on week on year?
S'ides drifting round the oceans it really isn't clear.
And if I ask that question to myself I find it hard,
To get an honest answer 'cos I'm always on my guard,
Against my lack of understanding, comprehension of this place,
The motives of the people that they call the human race.
So I go to sea to get away for peace and harmony
and I live at one with nature and leave land lubbers be.
My life is tough, I know it's rough but I've found my inner self,
And as long as I'm quite able and I'm lucky with my health,
I'll carry on regardless in search of what I find,
I'm just that sort of person, quite unique, one of a kind.

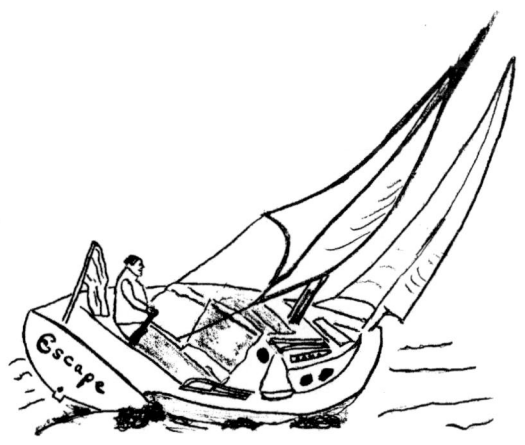

Dining in

Evening down the Drag-'em' Inn,
The owner thinks he's Cheng Man-ch'ing,
When I've had a long hard day
I like to eat a takeaway.
A chinky is my favourite food,
It puts me in a pleasant mood,
First pancake roll with lust devour
followed by the sweet & sour,
Then special rice and chicken ginger,
Food befitting of a ninja,
Makes me high from what I ate,
Mono Sodium Glutamate,
Wash it down with Saki wine,
Chinese food is so divine.

Oh I've got to get Fit

Oh I've got to get fit,
I was given a BMI test
I'm sure she pinched my shirt and vest,
The needle shot clean off the scale,
I willed it back to no avail.
She said it's very big of me,
To tackle my obesity,
I know I should have been born a whale.

Oh I've got to get fit
And this time I'm not going to quit,
In this space-age modern day,
I can't help feeling there'd be a way,
Without being classed a loafer,
To lie out prostrate on the sofa,
And shed my excess pounds away.
Somehow I've got to get fit.

Oh I've got to get fit,
Conscience took me to a gym,
Something I did on a whim,
Paid up all with good intention,
Cost me more than I can mention,
The thought of jogging round the town,
Wore me out so I'm lying down,
To rid me of my hypertension.
Somehow I'm going to get fit.

Yes I've got to get fit,
There's my neighbour on his bike,
Said I could borrow it if I like,
Could I even hope to straddle,
The razor blade they call a saddle,
It'd cause me an extreme reaction,
Working out on that contraption,
Somehow I've got to get fit.

So how am I going to get fit?
I could try to lose some weight,
By putting less upon my plate,
Sign up on a healthy course,
of special low-fat ketchup sauce,
Remove temptation from the house,
Adopt the diet of a mouse,
Reluctantly I've got to get fit.

Oh I need to get fit,
Doc says, take it slow to start,
And make it easy on my heart,
First try getting out of bed,
And walking to the shops instead
of wasting all my time away
in bed where I'd much rather lay.
Will I ever get fit?

The Misunderstanding of Marjorie Cleese

She wasn't renowned for her integrity or tact,
In fact sometimes nobody knew how she would react at all.
It was once a close call when she lost her job and was sacked.
Mad Marjorie, they called her that was after her arrest for rampaging through the town dressed in her dressing gown.
David Porter caught her and led her like a lamb to the slaughter off to jail.
People were scared so much she wasn't offered bail,
Such was life.
Well that was it in a nutshell.
The detail would come out later after the data had been processed.
Of course Marjorie thought she'd been fitted up and she wasn't impressed,
Stitched up good and proper they thought she was possessed.
Mad Marjorie, terrible name but it was always the same; she was never to blame,
No responsibility for her sanity, no vanity,
She was a common working girl and she knew it and used it
to her advantage but she blew it because she went too far, Ha Ha, but in the end she would have the last laugh.
They didn't know half of what she was capable of and would never know.
She wasn't daft at all but she took the fall,
All for the sake of keeping the peace she didn't need to crawl.
But David Porter didn't see it that way,
He knew her from ages back from the lack of discipline at school,
There wasn't a rule she hadn't broken but she was so cool,

She had a certain composure that's why they chose her, to make the disclosure
and stick it out, her neck that is and she thought why the heck should I do it?
But she did and she's glad that she did because as a kid she was always repressed.
Nobody thought she'd wreck the place then chase him through the streets in her
dressing gown.
But why that night, and what a night to pick a fight, the neighbours were alight
with fright.
What they didn't know and the CCTV footage later did show
was that Marjorie had been attacked and burgled in her own home.
The man she'd apprehended had been on bended
knees begging for his life confronted with a knife wielded by Marjorie Cleese.
He had learnt the hard way and in one way he was pleased he'd got away with it
and it hadn't gone any further.
When the others got there he had gone so all was not as it seemed.
In hindsight it was bad to have deemed Marjorie mad
and in some ways it was sad to have jumped to that conclusion,
Unaware of the intrusion it had all led to the illusion of her madness.
It was so easy to be led by what others had said,
And jump on the bandwagon without a shred of evidence.
All because of the way people thought she was.
Marjorie was eventually accepted back into the community with impunity,
She was exonerated and felt liberated with a certain immunity and as soon as he,
David that is, had set her free unequivocally made the apology.

The Village Pub

I love to go to the village pub and meet old friends of mine,
To prop up the bar and share a jar of beer or a glass of wine,
Just like old John, yes please John a pint of best,
He doesn't drink a lot, a pint and he's gone,
That's our John back to the nest and the missus,
Then there's Pete, the nicest guy you'll ever meet,
He's in for the night, thanks Pete I'll have a pint of the best,
Through the night it goes on and on, friends like John,
And Pete and Graham and Sue, who
live down the lane where Richard and Jane live,
And what I wouldn't give to live in their house,
Thanks Graham a pint of best, that goes down so well,
Now what was I saying? Oh yesh I was torkin abou mi fwens,
What a gweat brunch of preople, a pub is a meeetin prace,
Where yo can sup a pint or four before fallin on the floor,
While makin for the door of the gents and not findin it,
So the fence will av to do.
Ah that's better.
A pint of best Mike,
Ees the barman, im n Trish,
Now she's a dish, delish,
Well she was in er younger day,
And she couldn't arf play, knock the spots off those dominoes,
Woe betide anyone oo crossed her uh?
She wore the trousers, lovely rear, kept tabs on the beer,
Made sure it were clear, beautiful pint, the best,

That's why we keep coming back,
Then Jack takes us home, ee don't drink,
Ee just makes sure we do.
A little gold mine this place.
Right, off ome now,
Good night.

In Hindsight

Was that a pint of beer I saw
or was it in my mind,
Funny things seem to happen
when you're going blind.

My body's giving up on me
there's not a lot of it left,
Live bands, loud music and discotheque's,
Have left me rather deaf.

My liver's on its way out too,
The drink I drank too much,
It seems my way of living
was completely out of touch.

Don't mention that I'm over-weight
I know that I'm quite fat,
The curries and good living,
Influenced all of that.

I'm really now in quite a mess,
How long do you think I've got?
I hope to have a few more years,
Before my body's shot.

Three score and ten is average,
And that it is the best,
For someone in the state I'm in,
Before I'm laid to rest.

I've opted to be toasted,
It's nice and warm you know,
To be buried and get frosted,
Is not a way to go.

So when I'm gone and scattered
and really, truly dead,
Don't live the way I lived my life,
Go for the one hundred.

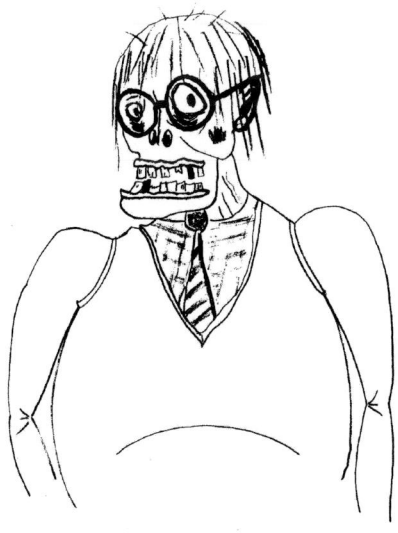

Second Thoughts

I wish I had chosen a different career,
My nerves are shot in less than a year,
A plumber, a baker, a building constructor,
Oh why did I choose a driving instructor?

Attracted by travel and a need to be free,
Cooped up in an office just wasn't for me,
I wanted a job with the world at my feet,
But all that I've got is the passenger seat,

Today is worse than it's been for a while,
We ran down three people in less than a mile,
"What pretty red lights" said one passing them by,
That was the point that I thought I would die,

My charitable feelings of teaching to drive,
Have now been replaced by my need to survive,
Lord give them strength when driving out later,
It was bad enough now on the simulator.

A Hole in One

I'm where you least expect me,
At a time that isn't right,
I've been waiting here quite hidden
in your shoe and out of sight.
And when you see me peeping
at you there between your toes,
All wide-eyed, white and gaping,
How I got there heaven knows.
Oh darn it!
Yes, I hear you say
and only if you would,
You'd save yourself embarrassment
let that be understood.
So take me off and change me
I am trying to console,
Your reconciliation with
your stocking with a hole.

Bionic Geriatricism

A handle for my handle, yes I think I'll call it Fred,
I grab it every morning it helps me out of bed,
I never needed one before it's new to me you know,
I've always had the strength before to get up and just go.

But now I'm getting older and these things I need to have,
Like the gadget in the toilet that is fitted to the lav,
My carer takes an interest in the things I do that hurt,
And she's there with a solution for the buttons on my shirt.

The kettles got a lever that I press to get a drink,
I've even got a gizmo to put the plug into the sink,
An adaptation designed for this and a gadget intended for that,
I've even got a funny device for extinguishing the cat.

I've now become robotic all my stuff has got a jig,
And I can't help now believing that I'm just a guinea pig,
For the companies that make them with the aim to help me out,
They save me lots of bother when I used to curse and shout.

Life has changed in so many ways I wonder where I am,
But some of them are so complicated I just can't give a damn,
And if I ever want something to move a tap that's stiff,
Then I phone the Social Services and they'll fit it in a jiff.

I'm a spoilt old pensioner whose movements are restricted,
The rheumatism and joint pain have left me so afflicted,
So let me count on you my friends the younger generation,
To help me through my senior years of increased age frustration

Spider

It's there,
In her hair,
The spider,
Do I tell her?
Will she care?

There's another,
Like the another,
Near her neck,
Ooo eck,
Oh brother.

She doesn't know,
Even so,
Do I tell?
Maybe,
Well,
Maybe no.

Happiness

Am I really that easy to please?
A glass of fine port and a chunk of blue cheese,
Not any blue cheese but a wedge of Castello,
Nothing is finer to render me mellow,
The port must have aged for a decade at least,
Clear as a bell and harbour a beast
of flavour all fit for a Lord in his manor,
And round it all off with a nice cool Havana.

Between the Posts

Rugby's not for nancys,
Those funny balls need skill,
The players like to shake your hand,
Then dive in for the kill,

They are the mighty fullbacks,
A ruthless crash of men,
They say their prayers before a game,
"Let's get em now" Amen.

They breed them like brick toilets,
Genetically engineered,
Descendants of Goliath,
And utterly revered.

Scrum down and up and under,
Pass a dummy and take a line,
They knock it on and pass it back,
You should see their eighty nine.

But off the field they're different,
They have a gracious side,
They seem to be quite normal,
Dr Jekyll and Mr Hyde.

They're your city gent, intelligent,
That wouldn't hurt a fly,
A banker who's a flanker,
When depositing a try.

So just you look about you,
There won't be one too far,
And when you find you're tackled,
It's because they know who you are.

Contentment

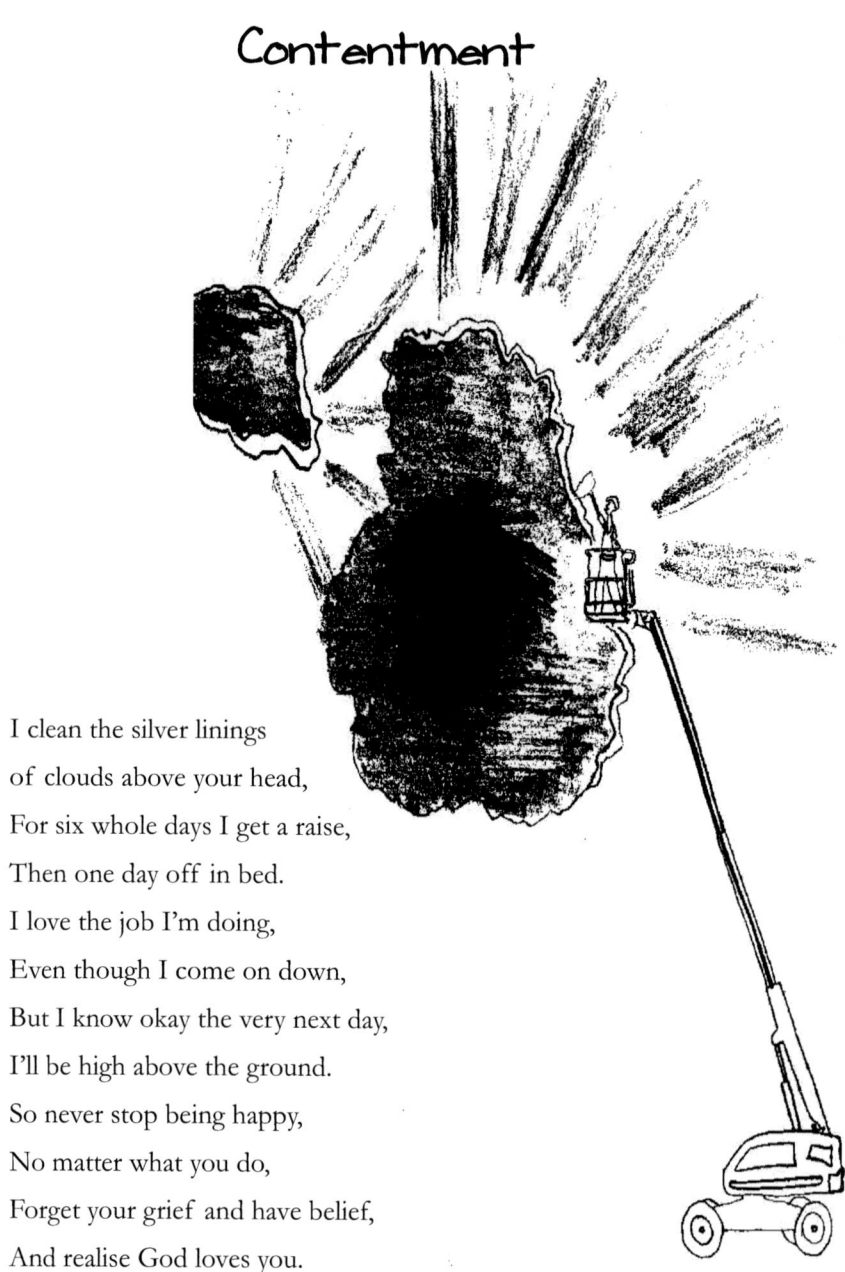

I clean the silver linings
of clouds above your head,
For six whole days I get a raise,
Then one day off in bed.
I love the job I'm doing,
Even though I come on down,
But I know okay the very next day,
I'll be high above the ground.
So never stop being happy,
No matter what you do,
Forget your grief and have belief,
And realise God loves you.

Caught in the Act

Said the wife to her friend I could have shot'em,
There they were in the grass when I caught'em
He said don't blame me,
She was stung by a bee,
And I was sucking the sting from her bottom.

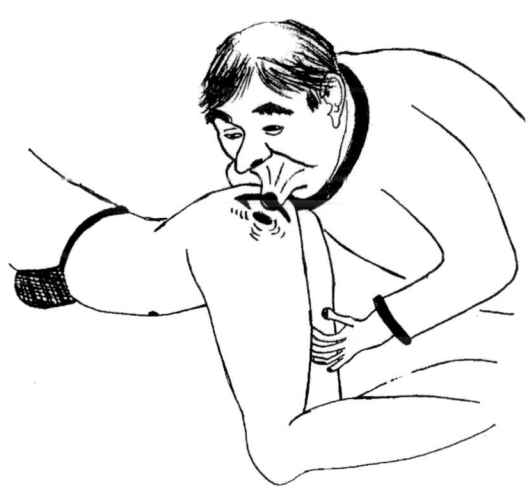

Ronald's New Mac

Ronald was flying on cloud nine,
He had the winning bid,
He always wanted a Burberry Mac,
Ever since he was a kid.

It was a long light brown coat,
With buttons and a belt,
He imagined how he'd wear it,
How it looked and how it felt.

He left very positive feedback,
To the seller on the web,
And couldn't believe it was once owned,
By a famous TV celeb.

When it arrived he put it on,
It fitted like a glove,
He wore it to the cinema,
Where he was sure that he'd find love.

He walked towards two ladies,
Who were ambling down the street,
And opened up his Burberry Mac,
To give them both a treat.

You're nicked so come with us sir,
We've been looking for you, Ah ha,
We're escorting you back to our place,
Are you up for a ménage à trois?

The Ageing Process

Why do the days get shorter?
Or is it in my mind,
That when the years get longer,
The less time do I find?
For doing what I want to,
Or being where I should,
If only I was able,
Or even if I could.

My mind is still quite active,
But I need to rest a lot,
With thoughts that are attractive,
Though I'm happy with what I've got.
I'm slower than I'm used to,
When jumping out a seat,
I have to check the floor is there,
When getting to my feet.

I'm getting very tired these days,
I now go to bed at nine,
There was a time I'd go all night
and the next day I'd be fine.
Now my days are numbered,
And I'm setting out my stand,
I hope that life is easier,
In the other land.

Couple of Show-offs

When our two cats play tennis,
They use the Alexander Technique,
They don't win many competitions,
But by gum it's improved their physique,

The crowds all flock to see them,
It's quite unusual you know,
To wear matching kit from Armani,
They end up stealing the show.

A Blind Date in Eden

Oh God why did you put me here,
What on earth did you have in mind?
Uncut grass and old fruit trees,
There's nothing else to find.

Not even a seat to sit on,
Just a fig leaf to my name,
What are you expecting from me?
It's not funny I hold you to blame.

This is a boring place to be,
No WIFI, bath or tele,
No corner shop or fast food joint,
To satisfy my belly.

But wait a sec who's that I see?
There's someone else what a relief,
Hey, hey she's winking back at me,
I think I need a larger leaf.

Forget about what I just said,
We're dining out tonight,
There's apple on the menu,
Then fig Angel Delight!

Raising an Eyebrow

I chanced upon an old eyebrow in our local charity shop,
I did considerer buying it but one eyebrow's not much cop,
It raised itself when it saw me as if to say I'm here,
And if I didn't know better I'd swear it shed a tear,
It was long and brown with a hint of grey in one of the hairs or two,
And it came with full instructions and a tube of super glue,
Now I have this nagging feeling eating at my brain,
There's no way I can leave it and not see it again,
So it joins me when I go out, it's even with me now,
My closest friend I can depend on Eric my cute eyebrow.

Neighbourhood

Old Mrs Pantzaroff, you'll never guess,
Went to the shops in a see through dress,
Her neighbour Mrs Jean O' Malley,
Said she's lost it, gone doolally,

That's what happened to Mr Jolly,
He went completely off his trolley,
Out in the rain without his brolly,
Died next day, what a wally.

You remember poor old Mrs Bain?
Started screaming, went insane,
Drank a case of Grand Champagne,
We never heard from her again.

Then going back a year or two,
That funny boy at thirty two,
Popping hormones, sniffing glue,
Now they keep him in the zoo.

And Mr Maheadoff strange old bloke,
Life to him was just a joke,
The men in white took him away,
Laughed himself to death they say.

I look at you and wonder why,
You think you're normal and deny,
Having foibles just like them,
Come divulge your own problem.

All Because the Lady Loves Chablis

There's a Lady I know loves Chablis,
"It slips down" she says, very happily,
By the fifth glass,
She's flat on her back,
'Cos the wine makes her legs go all wabbly.

Adolescence

My Mother told me when I was ten,
I'd be mature at twelve and then,
Hair would leap out of my chin,
From little pores within my skin,
Then spread around my mouth and cheeks,
And be a full blown beard in weeks,
On my shoulders down my arms,
Between my fingers on my palms,
Down my legs and on my toes,
At least an inch a day it grows,
"Oh Mum" I said, "don't be so daft,
I know you're joking, having a laugh".

Newton's Headache

Why let gravity pull you down,
Be happy and cheerful instead,
It wasn't the cause that made Newton frown,
But the apple's effect on his head.

I Love You so Much I Can't be Without You

I sit and watch the world go by,
I drink a beer and give a sigh,
I have a smoke and close one eye,
And sit and watch the world go by.

My girl walked out I don't know why,
She upped and left with no goodbye,
I feel so low that I could die,
I sit alone and cry and cry.

I want to tell the world that I,
Am such a lucky, happy guy,
She's back, she'd only been to buy,
Some veggies for tonight's stir fry.

Sharing Their Nuts

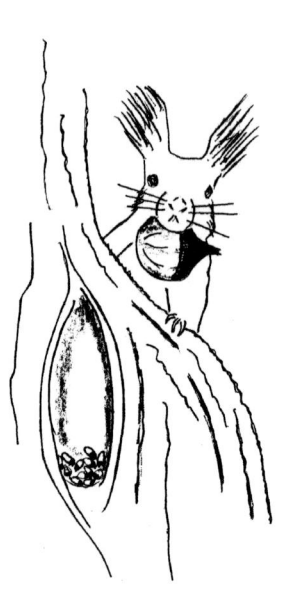

Two trees were talking in a wood,
Don't say it! You're thinking if they could?
Concerned about their acorns and
that blessed squirrel's sneaky hand.
Well what do'ya know he's got some guts,
To come and nibble at our nuts,
I'm not so bothered as it stands,
At least he hasn't got cold hands,
Two aged old oaks just standing there,
Quite happy for their nuts to share.

Naive

When I was young and quite naive,
What grown-ups said I did believe,
My Uncle told me of his pet,
The one he got, I hadn't met,
It was a monkey young and shy,
And hid from people passing by,
It had been seen, a fleeting glance,
Can I see it any chance?
You can see it clear as day,
In the mirror he would say.

Old Jake

At his friends the other day,
Rupert and his old dog Jake,
Were sitting chatting in the lounge,
With a cup of tea and slice of cake.

Come and see the garden pond,
The dog's asleep so leave the door,
But when returning to the lounge,
The slice of cake was there no more.

Rupert wailed! "My cake has gone."
And looked around accusingly,
Old Jake still flat out on the floor,
Twitched an eyelid knowingly.

"Where's my cake for goodness sake,"
Old innocence stretched out a paw,
"You naughty dog" he scolded Jake,
The evidence all round his jaw.

Food Power

If I eat my carrots can I see in the dark?
If I finish my spinach can I wrestle a shark?
If I eat all my crusts will my hair grow curly?
If I don't eat sweets will my teeth stay pearly?
If I don't eat my fish will my knowledge be trimmed?
If I eat my baked beans can I run like the wind?

Sweet Treat

Please give me some more of your hot spotted dick,
All lavishly covered with cream nice and thick,
It fills me up beautifully I can't get enough,
It's almost as good as my great gran's plum duff.

Jack + Jill

Jack said, "Jill now you're on the pill",
Shall we? Do you think we ought'a?
In the eiderdown Jill's Dad came round,
Said "what are you doing with my daughter"?

Donation

Of all the people in the world,
There's only one of me,
I work to help the limbless,
And aid mobility.

I'm based out in the country,
I'm not out there by chance,
The factory's near the river,
In a rural part of France.

My job is very special,
I'm always in demand,
Making lightweight wheelchairs,
I keep a lot on hand.

I make them by the dozen,
Green ones sell the best,
Manual or electric,
Come put them to the test,

The users come in bus loads,
We're on a popular route,
You can buy the ready-made ones,
Or we make them up to suit.

The French are quite discerning,
We're a victim of their taste,
They seem to really like us,
Well, the bits below the waist.

It is a growing business,
Sometimes a long backlog,
There's really no alternative,
To help a legless frog.

A Golden Opportunity

What more has life to offer me? I'm fed up with this race,
I'd like to get away from it and find a quieter place,
I read the Sunday paper once and in the back I saw,
An ad to learn prospecting, well I couldn't ask for more.

A chance to get away from my jobs chaos and its noise,
To spend some time in solitude soaking up the joys
of getting back to nature and living life as one,
With all the beautiful creatures that live beneath the sun.

How my mouth is watering at the thought of all that bliss,
Remembering all the people that I know I wouldn't miss,
So bring it on this change of life I desperately desire,
And all the perfect qualities of life I will acquire.

So it's off for gold I'm going and a chance of getting lucky,
Expecting good conditions not the thought of getting mucky,
Panning for those nuggets in a cool clear mountain stream,
What the hell!
The fire bell,
Oh it's good sometimes to dream.

Sunshine for Health

In the sunflower part of the garden,
At the hottest time of day,
I catch sunbeams in bottles
and I store them safley away.

Then in the dark of winter,
I set my sunbeams free,
To bring some sunshine in my life
and to get my vitamin D.

Going Nowhere

I've bought a classic car,
It is the coolest ever,
The seats are made of leather,
It's an E-Type jaguar. Ja.*

I'm rolling out my ride,
Take it for a spin,
Don't ask me where I've bin,
It won't be very far.

The engines just cut out,
It made a cough and splutter,
There are round things in the gutter,
It makes me want to shout. OUT.

I'm sitting on the grass,
Waiting for the man,
The AA yellow van,
An' got a cold damp ass. Blast.

I wish I'd bought a bike,
It would have been less stress,
I wouldn't be in this mess,
I think that's what I'd like.

(Yes in German pronounced Yah)

Settling Down

When I decide to settle down,
I have a girl in my mind,
I'll pick a chick from out of town,
That has a nice behind.

She'll stand out from the other girls,
As any girl won't suit me,
I need a very special girl,
A gorgeous little cutie.

I'll love her till the end of time,
She'll never want to stray,
By that time I'll be in my prime,
Distinguished old and grey.

Fish Wife

I'm a common old English fish wife,
Who hasn't had much of a life,
I cut and scale the fish by day
and have a gossip,
By the way.

You know of her at forty four?
I saw her with that bloke next door,
In a compromising pose,
Doing something with a hose.

Telling porkies nah, not me,
Just sharing out the things I see,
I like to know what's going on,
And so do you, so now come-on?

I'm a foul mouthed English fish wife,
I shout and curse all my life,
To me there is no other way,
I love a gossip,
By the way,

You know the blond haired skinny bloke,
I reckon he's been sniffing coke,
He had white powder on his clothes,
From that rave up I suppose.

Scandal in our community?
There's nothing much that gets past me.

Holiday of a Lifetime

What have you got in those cases?
They weigh a ton and a half,
If you reckon you'll get them on aboard?
They'll think that you're having a laugh,

A holiday of a lifetime we called it,
It took ages to save up the money,
Together we booked all the tickets,
Now we're off to the warm and the sunny.

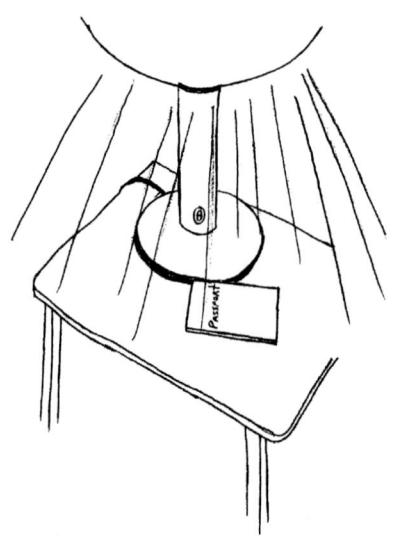

The journey to Heathrow took ages,
The bus and the train overnight,
We eventually got to the airport,
In the grey of the morning light.

We're very excited we're going,
And I'm hoping that I am still able,
I wish I was home at the moment,
'Cos my passport was left on the table.

Gran'd Exit

Am I the only kid around?
Haunted by that roaring sound,
Again she's got her right foot down,
And burning up the town.

She joined the local hooligans,
Why can't she be like other Nans,
Knitting quietly with her hands,
A Gran like other veterans.

I know she does it just for fun,
She thinks she's driving formula one,
At seventy five the son of a gun,
She's acting out her last home run.

Lest she lost it, one last dash,
Went in style a massive crash,
Tank caught fire and in a flash,
Thirty seconds she was ash.

Summer Lottery

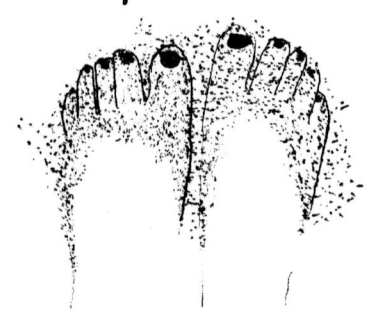

I love the smell of Summer,
Fresh grass smells up my nose,
The sunshine and the seaside,
The sand between my toes.

At home and in the Summer sun,
Really not concerned,
I have a lot of carefree fun,
Get red and badly burned.

We're eating in the garden,
A pleasant situation,
What's that funny smell?
Oh, the dogs got constipation.

And when the sun goes down,
I like a moonlight dance,
Now where'd I put my wine?
Struth! It's full of ants.

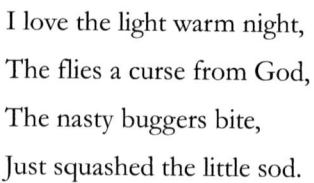

I love the light warm night,
The flies a curse from God,
The nasty buggers bite,
Just squashed the little sod.

This year we went abroad,
Destination Spain,
More than we could afford,
And all week we got rain.

So I'm counting on next Summer,
With keen anticipation,
Not to be a bummer,
I need a good vacation.

Oh the Wind

Why is it that fresh fruit and veg have side effects on me?
Five and six and seven a day I eat quite healthily,
Discretion in emission whilst in public is an art,
And if I can't control it I get up and just depart.

Bacon

Why oh why are our taste buds ach'n,
Our noses are twitch'n, and legs are shak'n,
Cold turkey at the merest whiff,
A lovely niff the smell of bacon.

Load us the butties, a sarnie that's plain,
As long as we taste that bacon again,
It's more than a food to an old carnivore,
A Sunday breakfast we all adore.

Retribution

Tommy Tucker little, rebel,
Double whisky then a treble,
Got into an awful fight,
Nursed his wounds all through the night.

Loves his drink from when he wakes,
Beer for breakfast on his flakes,
Everyday completely plastered,
Yes he's just a drunken, youth.

They call him slugger the little, tyrant,
In his mind he is a giant,
Such a selfish attitude,
Evil boy immensely rude.

Bullied all the kids at school,
Thought that he was oh so cool,
A rotten liar, double crosser,
Nothing but a stupid, idiot.

A bruiser from another place,
Tried to rearrange his face,
The hated rival took a swing,
He'd met his match how that did sting.

Full of rage he bit the dirt,
On the floor and he was hurt,
Begged for mercy not a bit,
Serves him right the little, hooligan.

The moral is that you'll be bound,
By what you sow it all comes round,
There's nowhere you can run or hide,
Living on the shady side.

Geri's Outing to Blackpool

Clutching blue bottles of Milk of Magnesia,
Trying to look busy attempting to hide their amnesia,
They've forgotten what they're doing, forgotten where they are,
In fact forgotten everything what a life, bizarre,

Nowhere to sit in the breakfast room?
Wasting time for the sake of it, that's clear,
Hoping that Elvis will appear
and entertain them with a song from the war years.

Stiletto's on toast,
Old tarts and farts make the most
of their weekend astray with an extra day,
That clinched the deal, that's why they're away.

A real English breakfast, what a spread,
They said it would do us proud,
Applaud the chef and the waitresses too,
The stick-on smile there just for you,
It's the annual getaway all aboard,
A low-cost weekend they can all afford.

They're all well past it

Halloween Madness

It was a dark and stormy night
and goodly folk were sleeping,
While ghoulies were a creeping
and watching eyes were peeping,
Someone turn on the light,
I can't stand this much longer,
The feelings getting stronger,
That something isn't right.

Did you hear that scream?
I think that someone's dying,
Or is it someone crying?
The Devils started frying,
It could be all a dream,
I can't take this much more,
There's blood upon the floor,
I suppose its Halloween.

It's a dark and stormy night,
The evils in my head,
I know the neighbours dead,
I locked her in the shed,
To get her out of sight,
Who's rapping at my knocker?
I'm going off my rocker,
I need to see some light.

They've come to cart me off,
There's been a few complaints,
I'm strapped up in restraints,
They think that they are saints.
You may sit there and scoff,
I've had enough of this,
Aware of what's amiss
I know when I'm well off.

Justice on the Rebound

Robin De-Rich was a scoundrel and thief,
A likeable rogue with morals amiss,
A nuisance to folk who had lots of money,
A wanted villain in the eyes of police.

Thieving was fun he did it in style,
He'd tickle them silly and have them in stitches,
There on the floor they'd be giggling and laughing while,
Robin would lift all their money and riches.

The funny thing was they liked it so much,
They hadn't a clue of what had gone on,
Distracted completely by his clever touch,
Laying there chuckling Robin had gone.

The Sheriff was livid we can't have this clown,
Robbing our people he's got to be caught,
He sent out his deputies all over town,
Calming the people who were clearly distraught.

A sovereign was offered for good information,
To capture the renegade and put him in jail,
His actions were that of a bad generation,
He'd never get out or even get bail.

When he was caught the streets were heaving,
They brought him in publicly tethered and bound,
Some were supporters others were grieving,
People had gathered from miles around.

The sheriff accused him of robbing and pinching,
This method of taking had never been known,
Don't be surprised if you're in for a lynching,
What you have done we can never condone.

Up went the scaffold some weeks later,
Everything there except for the rope,
The trap-door was tested, perfectly working,
Was this the end, was there no hope?

The rope isn't ready it's still in the making,
Try over there, the Adventure Club's chest,
Pick out a good one we don't want it breaking,
Bring the yellow one it's by far the best.

Now was the time the moment had come,
The trap-door was sprung poor Robin went down,
Audible gasps were heard from the cheap seats,
Ladies with hankies in tears all around.

Up through the trap-door shot Robin the convict,
The people all cheered they'd given up hope,
He loosened the noose and made a quick exit,
They'd used the Adventure Clubs bungee rope.

Table Differences

From a chaps' point of view,
The result is nothing new,
Washing up just doesn't pay,
Use a clean plate every day,
Throw away the dirty one,
Convenient, tidy and loads of fun.

From a ladies' point of view,
The colour is the clue,
Set the table, candle light,
Wash and dry up every night,
To have a set of eight is neat,
Just in case friends come to eat.

Miss Broken Hart

Marigold Hart was the local tart,
Dressed to the nines and looking the part,
She hung round the boys with their fancy toys
playing loud music and making a noise.
Her hair changed its colour three times a week
and her clothes were so tight that her bottom would squeak,
She'd speak in a high voice with eyes like a lamb,
Pretty nice girl though gram for gram.
A very nice girl in a strange sort of way,
You couldn't help want her at least for a day,
and if you did she's sure to demolish ya,
She's stroked more wood than a furniture polisher.

Not the Way

Take next right, no sign of a turning,
Navigational signals definitely not working,
I thought this thing was there to know,
Where I programmed it to go.

I'm heading west it thinks its east,
Surely it knows that at least,
That little man up in the sky,
Doesn't know the reason why.

Quickest, shortest it would say,
I can't be bothered either way,
As long as I arrive today,
Or I know there'll be hell to pay.

I bought this thing to help me out,
And all I seem to do is shout,
Advised by that young sales assistant,
I now know why he was persistent.

It doesn't work, it cost a bomb,
What country did they say it's from?
Nothing but a waste of space,
A firing squad it's going to face.

Winding back the sunroof I,
Toss the Sat Nav to the sky,
I watch it float for just a second,
It's got what it deserves I reckoned.

Useless thing, electronic faeces,
Smashed into a thousand pieces,
I'll use my map to find direction,
A better way upon reflection.

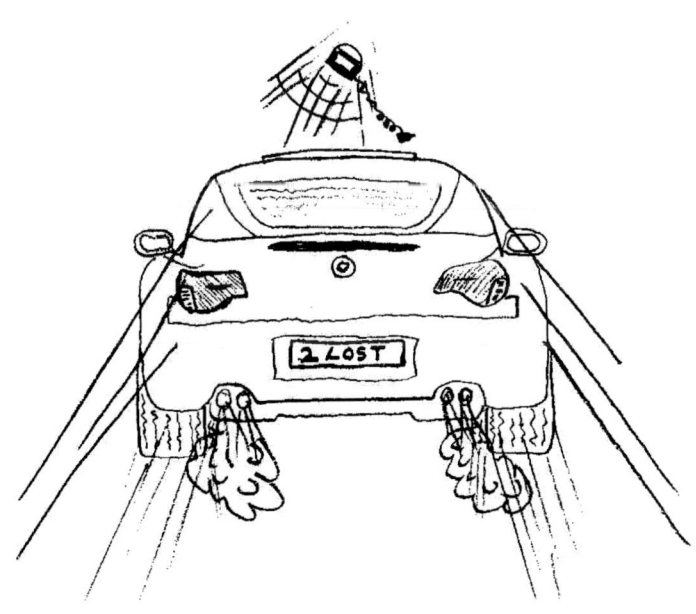

Life in School

Young blue whales as a rule,
Never need to go to school,
For in a school they'll always be,
When they're with their family.

Scrambled Egg on Toast

A golden wholemeal toasted slice,
With melting butter to entice,
Three free range eggs all beaten up,
With a fork in a cup.

Tease them slowly round a pan,
Keep them moving best you can,
Set them out upon a plate,
Herbs on top to decorate.

Admire the art in your creation,
Formed with love a true sensation,
Cut in pieces to despatch,
Through the lips and down the hatch.

Not All There

Half a yard above the ground,
Floats a man without a sound,
He claims his legs are there alright,
But to us they're out of sight,
The top of him was plain to see,
As bold as brass to you and me,
But sticking out his underwear,
Clearly there was nothing there.

Something held him off the ground,
But nothing obvious could be found,
They're phantom legs I think they're neat,
Said a girl from up the street,
Do you think you'd be hard put
to let me see your phantom foot?
He said you'll see my phantom toe
if you don't naff off and go.

Another voice within the crowd
started shouting very loud,
He's not all there, a proper man,
Half the person that I am,
Yet here you are and seeming well,
Your bottom half prey come on tell,
Was it stolen lost maybe
in some awful tragedy?

We really are quite amused,
But then again somewhat bemused,
To see a person legless here,
Did you guzzle too much beer?
Holding back a stifled choke,
From laughing at his tasteless joke,
Silence struck a wild stampede
of disappearing tumbleweed.

He's a freak have him arrested,
Taken to a lab and tested,
Try to find what's going on
and where his lower parts have gone,
He's scaring people see that's clear,
There's something wrong, the atmosphere
is thick and now affecting folk,
Come get a grip upon this bloke.

The police said that he's here from space,
A planet from a far off place,
He's only trying to dress like us
and couldn't understand the fuss
about the bit below the waist
he'd forgotten in his haste.
Then while we watched him floating there,
He disappeared into thin air.

A Dogs Dream of Winning the Lottery

Have my numbers come up yet?
I'm completely fed up of working,
To get up early every day,
When in my bed I'd rather lay,
I'm sure that sleeps my greatest asset.

Oh, but to try it out,
Would encourage calls of idleness,
All the same I'd give it a go,
Just to find out, then I'd know,
What being lazy's all about?

Going Fishing

Amidst dense mist on a deserted beach,
With spades in hand digging the sand,
Lugworms for bait, Mark and his mate,
Were excited and relishing the thought of the fishing.

Dressed up warm on this early morn,
Skipping the dunes humming their tunes,
Two boys at play planning their day,
No school today it was Saturday.

Who'll catch the biggest announcing the contest,
Having a bet then? I'll beat you no sweat,
Back to the pier with the rods and the gear,
And a pack-up their Mums made and a flask of hot soup.

Their catch safely loaded each other they goaded,
Who'd caught the largest reliving the sport,
Today was such fun being out in the sun,
They couldn't help run, all the way home.

Time for Nothing

I set my alarm for 2 AM
and leapt up out of bed,
It's dark outside, the middle of the night,
I go downstairs turn on the light
and shake my weary head.

What shall I do with this time
that really doesn't exist?
I'll have a tea and sit awhile,
For what I do must be worthwhile,
I'll make myself a list.

In my chair I lean right back,
My mind is half asleep,
I know it's late and in my state,
I find it hard to concentrate,
I end up counting sheep.

Sixty minutes have gone by
my brain is almost dead,
The clocks went back, this extra hour
of being useful has gone sour,
I'm going back to bed.

Endorsed by Larva

There are maggots in the cheese again,
It's well and truly ripe,
I didn't think that Camembert
was a maggot's type?

Just brush them off its still ok,
It all adds to the flavour,
There's only about a dozen of them,
The plein de saveurs you'll savour.

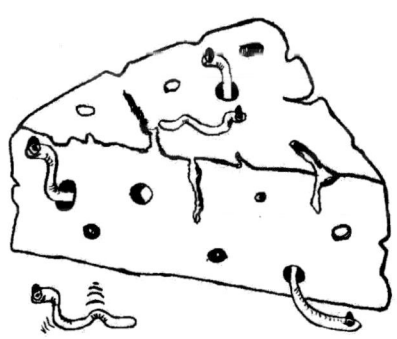

Divine Light

It's Sunday morning bright and fair
with Christians heading off to mass,
Lining pews all singing where
sunbeams pierce stained window glass.

In the pulpit Father John
is preaching of the divine light,
Reading Genesis from the Bible
how we got our day and night.

The congregation were bewildered
as he spoke a light appeared,
Dancing on the roof above them,
Intervention many feared.

At that time Miss Sheila Blige
had dropped her hymn book on the floor,
Bending over to retrieve it
exposed her shiny round contour.

Father look! That lights reflected,
See it how it jumps and flickers,
The good Lord chose the path projected,
Bouncing off Miss Sheila's knickers.

I'm Fired

It's my dream, what I was born for,
All my life it's what I've worked hard for,
I'm the son of a gun and I love getting fired,
I do all the fêtes and I'm regularly hired.

It blows my mind to be flying through air,
A bolt from the blue and a feeling I share
with a missile in flight crooning the earth,
Giving my all for what I am worth.

I'm a human cannonball shot from a gun,
It's not just a job but lots of fun,
Till those on the ground tripled the charge
of the powder that launches me way too large.
A mistake can happen anyone's fault,
It increased my range to a thunder bolt.

Long pause

Returning back from Sweden, I caught the fastest train,
By now I'd had quite enough of flying yet again,
So I'm grounded now and happy that my feet are firmly planted,
On the terra firma not exactly how I planned it,
I'll be airborne soon please go outside and look into the sky,
You never know it might be me you see go shooting by.

Pushing the Wrong Button

In an old garage messing around,
You wouldn't believe the stuff that we found,
Things from the past and next doors dead cat,
Old bits of this and loads of old tat,
Beneath it all a white tumble drier,
And inside the drum a broken fat fryer,
Stuff that had reached the end of its life,
Used kitchen pans and a blunt carving knife.
Then my friend Dave bravado and brave,
Stuck his head in a microwave,
Pressing the button as though for a joke,
It didn't light up so he thought it had broke,
What happened next I'll give you one guess?
We're all having counselling for post trauma stress.

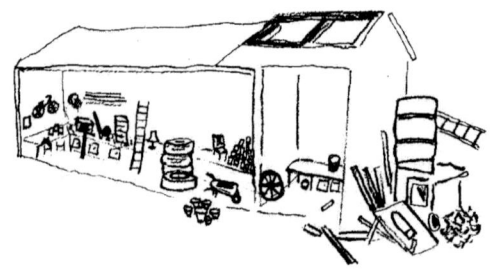

Did you Know?

Do you know?
I thought you knew,
The question caught me unawares,
I wasn't expecting an inquisition,
Especially from you.
I didn't talk to anyone,
It's sort of private you see,
So will you drop the matter
and please just let it be?
It wasn't only one or two of them,
Everyone wanted to know,
They thought that it was common place,
It was nothing and ages ago,
The whole thing seemed to escalate,
I was the talk of the town,
It never ceases to amaze me
how quick the word gets round.
But in the end I let bits out,
You know that tall young waiter,
Now you now know what it's about,
I'll give you details later.

Hopping the Boards

"Break a leg,"
First night she said,
I broke a leg,
I'm now in bed.

Juliet, Juliet where art thou Juliet? Come tend me.

Sport for All

Helmut Goodlicker was thought to be the best,
And was off to the Olympics to compete against the rest,
When he was rejected he left and took the hump,
Officials at the office said, "Go take a run and jump",

He decided to protest and asked for more support,
To recognise his talent and to show what he was taught,
There's never been a sport like this he openly admits,
And if you do it wrong you lose your thong and do the splits.

A valued second opinion was sought by all that played,
The outcome was unfavourable the members were dismayed,
All that time and effort, dedication gone to waste,
The judges ruled without a doubt, the sport was in bad taste.

How Much Longer Jim?

We were getting a bit concerned,
Nobody else gave a damn,
He's not on a diet,
Unless he's kept quiet,
He's just polished off half the ham.
Uncle Jim was always slim,
But we never thought him as thin,
Every week he'd come round for Sunday dinner,
All that food he ate and he's getting thinner,
He's the first to finish always the winner,
So why was he losing weight?

I had a quiet word in his ear,
And sent him off up to the Doc,
To see if he knew,
Or could hazard a clue,
What I heard was a bit of a shock.
He's certainly not getting smaller,
In fact he's eight inches taller,
He lies in his bed; he sticks out his leg,
Too lazy to rise and switch it instead,
Well that is the reason the doctor said,
Then turns off the light in the hall.

So he's not losing weight it's a myth,
He's such a lazy old git,
He should have predicted,
What he has inflicted,
He's over stretched just a bit.
So why did he not say a word,
The situation's absurd,
To us he was always good old Jim,
But now he's like a piece of string,
Nothing but a coiled up spring,
And nothing's changed I've heard.

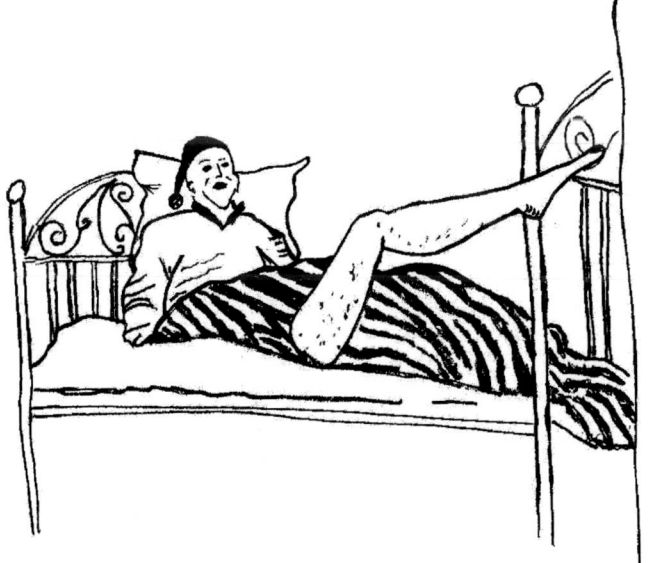

Inheritance

My life has not been easy,
A struggle through and through,
To earn sufficient money,
To care for all of you.

I wish I'd had the time,
To live life for myself,
It was a dream of mine,
Way up upon a shelf.

I hope I manage something,
Or all this is in vain,
I tell you if this happens,
I'm coming back again.

So you lot just remember,
Where you got your cash,
Go invest it wisely,
Don't blow it all on hash.

Epilogue

When you've finished this one,
Please turn the page and look,
That's why I called it epilogue,
The last one in the book.

If you enjoyed the reading
Don't let this be the end,
Go and buy another one
and give it to a friend.

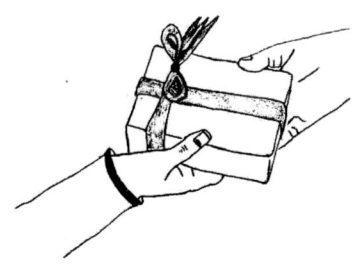

INDEX OF FIRST LINES

A golden wholemeal toasted slice 133
A good shag in the morning.. 6
A handle for my handle yes I think I'll call it Fred 80
Although my home was no bigger than a box................................ 66
Am I really that easy to please?.. 83
Am I the only kid around?.. 115
Amidst dense mist on a deserted beach 137
Andrew was a Brylcreem boy a product of the fifties................... 4
Arid, scorched almost beyond hydration...................................... 54
At his friends the other day... 102

Before I was evicted... 37
Break a leg.. 144

Can I take your order sir?... 7
Can you lend me a quid Sid?... 16
Clutching blue bottles of Milk of Magnesia.............................. 122

Do you know? 143

Evening down the Drag-'em' Inn.. 68

From 16 to 60 I paid my tax.. 9
From a chaps point of view 128
Funny thing l'ectricity.. 29

Giz a fag I'm gasping an I really an't a clue................................. 10
Going back a year or two.. 32

Half a yard above the ground 134
Harry the fish they called him... 30
Have my numbers come up yet?... 136
He opened one hand then the other.. 48
Helmut Goodlicker was thought to be the best........................ 145

- Index of First Lines -

I am the intrepid sailor and I cruise the open sea 67
I chanced upon an old eyebrow in our local charity shop 93
I clean the silver linings 86
I don't have to tell you what happened next 2
I don't know why I do it 25
I love the smell of summer 116
I love to go to the village pub and meet old friends of mine 74
I set my alarm for 2 AM 138
I sit and watch the world go by 99
I wish I had chosen a different career 78
I'm a common old English fish wife 112
I'm not sure if it's fact or rumour 20
I'm where you least expect me 79
I've bought a classic car 110
If I eat my carrots can I see in the dark? 103
If I were an ant 13
I'm off to get my hair cut 52
In an old garage messing around 142
In the sunflower part of the garden 109
It doesn't matter just how gently 26
It happened oh so quickly 61
It was a dark and stormy night 124
It was a lovely evening so we chose to have a meal 46
It's careless really, quite remiss 60
It's my dream, what I was born for 141
It's Sunday morning bright and fair 140
It's there 82

Jack said, "Jill now you're on the pill" 105
John never knew what hit him 38
John would look in the mirror and stare 22

Laying in bed on a cold Sunday morn 42
Laying on a red seat 31

- Index of First Lines -

M'mmm the whiff of chips	44
Madam Zarla runs the hoopla at the local fair	45
Marigold Hart was the local tart	129
Max Casson was a stoker	18
Mona had a good voice she was an auctioneer	15
My body now has had enough	43
My friend Jim's an alligator	59
My life has not been easy	148
My Mother told me when I was ten	97
Never let it not be said	28
Of all the people in the world	106
Oh God why did you put me here	92
Oh I've got to get fit	69
Old Mrs Pantzaroff, you'll never guess	94
On a cold and frosty winters night	14
Outside in the cold and naked	53
Please give me some more of your hot spotted dick	104
Quasi met Esmeralda at the annual cathedral fête	40
Reach high, touch the sky	12
Robin De-Rich was a scoundrel and thief	126
Ronald was flying on cloud nine	88
Rugby's not for Nancy's	84
Said the wife to her friend I could have shot'em	87
She wasn't renowned for her integrity or tact	72
St. Michael they all called me	39
Suddenly our cat's a spring chicken	55
T' was Tuesday at the end of May	34
Take next right, no sign of a turning	130

- Index of First Lines -

The dark and white a lovely sight, a sneaky bite to eat at night............ 1
The dark of the night and all is still.. 47
The man with the moustache 56
Their love could not be stronger... 49
There are maggots in the cheese again... 139
There's a Lady I know loves Chablis 96
Tommy Tucker, little rebel 120
Two trees were talking in a wood.. 100

Was that a pint of beer I saw... 76
We were getting a bit concerned 146
What have you got in those cases?.. 114
What more has life to offer me? I'm fed up with this race...................... 108
When I decide to settle down... 111
When I was a baby I couldn't talk... 21
When I was young and quite naive 101
When in the midday sun.. 41
When our two cats play tennis.. 91
When you've finished this one 149
Where's me umbrella I had it in me hand... 11
Who'll give me 50 57
Why do the days get shorter?.. 90
Why is it that fresh fruit and veg have side effects on me?..................... 118
Why let gravity pull you down?... 98
Why oh why are our taste buds ach'n... 119
Wow just made it, come on Nic that's our table over there 8

Young blue whales as a rule 132